SEEKING STANLEY

THE ELUSIVE SEARCH FOR THE MICHAEL STANLEY BAND

A Self-Indulgent Novel
By
Timothy Giles

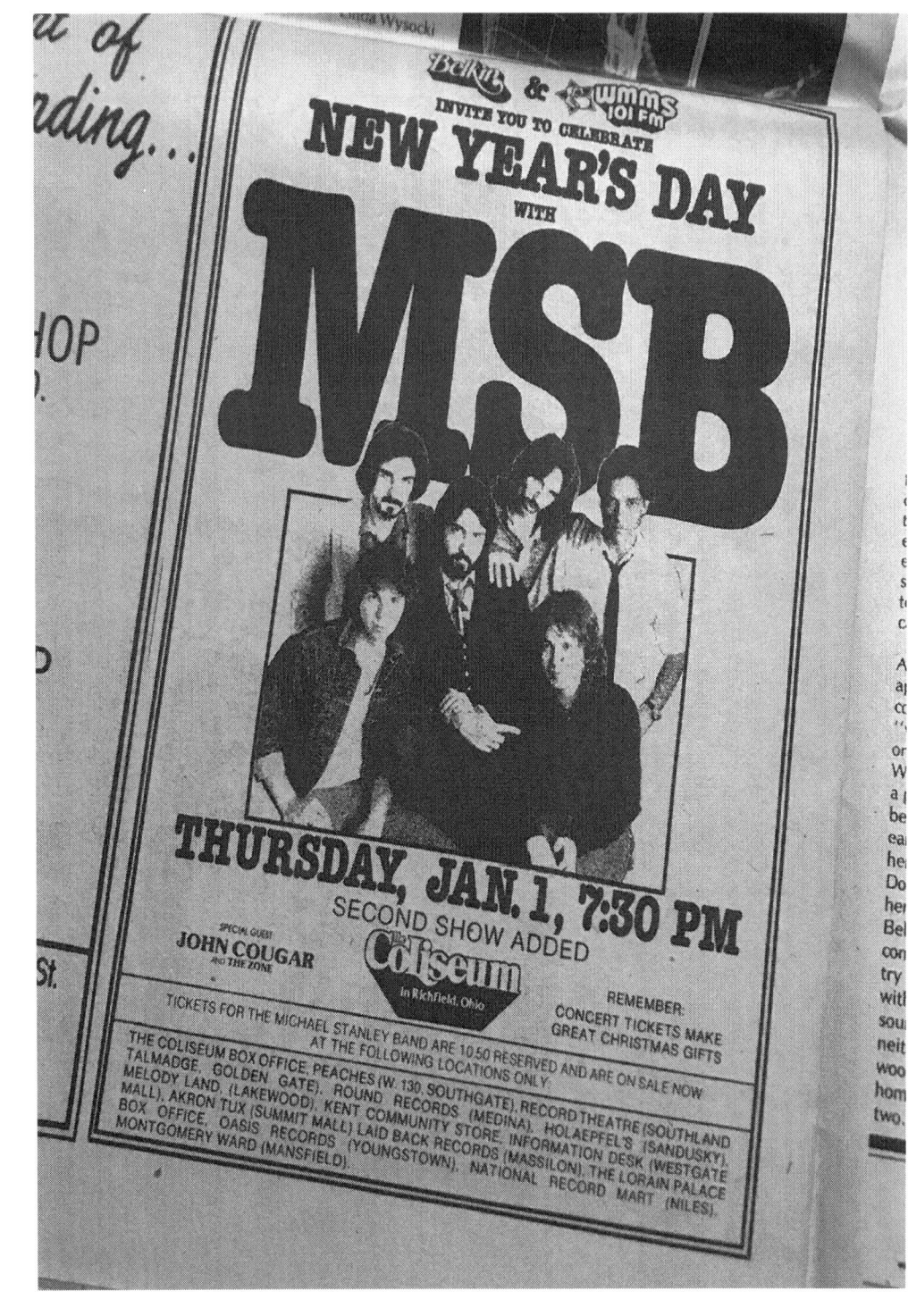

Contents

What The Hell Is This All About?..13
Chapter One 14
   Who Is The Michael Stanley Band?????????.............................14
Chapter Two..17
   The Technology Dark Ages 17
Chapter Three...23
   The Mall, Sam Goody, And Where Is Heartland??? 23
Chapter Four...26
   High School Heroes No One Ever Heard Of..................................26
Chapter Five..29
   Slippery Rock University And Pittsburgh......................................29
Chapter Six..42
   April 26, 1986, A New Date That Would Live In Infamy. 42
Chapter Seven 50
   Let's Get The Show On The Road 50
Chapter Eight..61
   What's Next For Me And Msb??? 61
Chapter Nine 74
   THE INTERNET BRINGS TOGETHER...............................74
   THE FAITHFUL 74
Chapter 10...86
   Will The Ride Continue?..86
Chapter 11……………………………………………………………91
We Sing With Our Heroes……………………………………………..91

MICHAEL STANLEY BAND

Morrow Field House
Sunday, March 6

Tickets go on sale Monday, Feb. 14, 1983 at 8:30 a.m.

For student with SRSC ID

Ten ticket limit on the first day. Cash only

CU Ticket booth and *for Gen. Public*, Tues. Feb. 15, 1983

for More Info Contact The College Union At 794-7535

Still sealed after all these years.

The Famous Heartland Bowl/Coaster Set.

Stanley and Raleigh Blossom July 1986

Motely Crue??? Billy Squire??

Never heard of them!!!!!!!!!!!!!!!!!!!!!!!

Dick Clark's favorite band

All graphics included in this work have all been procured via the public domain and the internet.

© 2021 Timothy A. Giles (timothyagiles@hotmail.com) Feel free to contact me with any comments. Thanks in advance for reading.

All rights reserved, including the right to reproduce this book or portions thereof in any form whatsoever.

All lyrics quoted within this work by Michael Stanley and Kevin Raleigh

Second edition (and most likely last edition)

WHAT THE HELL IS THIS ALL ABOUT?

If you are reading this, then something about the title or the quest to locate MSB peaked your interest in regard to my fixation during the 1980's and later for my Heartland Rock musical heroes. Being a quiet, actually quite a book worm, history buff during my teen years, it's hard to fathom that I had any interest at all in popular music. But this story in all its factual glory is 100% true and has been brewing inside me for years and finally needed an outlet and be told to the masses (if anyone will actually read this).

Since that day in the Fall of 1981, my musically appreciation and admiration of 2 guitars, vocals and drums has increased quite dramatically. If it wasn't for Bruce Springsteen, Little Steven, Bob Seger, The Who, and of course the Michael Stanley Band, you would be looking at blank pages or someone else's obsession.

This is dedicated to my wife Donna Marie, who has endured the MSB obsession for 25 years and of course Matthew Miami, the Living Proof of our life.

CHAPTER ONE
WHO IS THE MICHAEL STANLEY BAND?????????

Michael Stanley (born March 25, 1948 as Michael Stanley Gee in Cleveland, Ohio) is an American singer-songwriter, musician, and radio personality. Both as a solo artist and with the Michael Stanley Band, his brand of heartland rock was popular in Cleveland and around the American Midwest in the 1970s and 1980s.

The Michael Stanley Band was formed by Stanley in 1974 with singer-songwriter–lead guitarist Jonah Koslen, former Glass Harp bassist Daniel Pecchio and drummer Tommy Dobeck from the band Circus. There were several personnel changes over the years and by 1982 the group had evolved into a seven-piece band.

Nicknamed MSB by their fans, the band set several attendance records at Cleveland area venues including a record 20,320 at the Richfield Coliseum on July 20, 1979[4] and a record 40,529 for two Coliseum concerts on December 31, 1981 and January 1, 1982. The band's greatest achievement was a total attendance of 74,404 during a four-night stand at Blossom Music Center on August 25, 26, 30 and 31, 1982.[5]

The group reached the peak of their popularity nationally in 1981 when the single "He Can't Love You" from the album *Heartland* (written and sung by keyboardist Kevin Raleigh) made the Top 40 (#33 *Billboard*, #27 *Cash Box*) and "In the Heartland" from the album *North Coast* went to #6 on Billboard's Top Tracks chart. Their video for "He Can't Love You" was the 47th video ever played on MTV.[6] The band's last Top 40 hit was "My Town" in 1983.

The band called it quits in 1986 with a series of twelve farewell shows at the Front Row Theatre during the 1986–87 holiday season

- Michael Stanley – guitar, vocals
- <u>Jonah Koslen</u> – lead guitar, vocals (1974–77)
- <u>Daniel Pecchio</u> – bass, vocals (1974–79)
- Tommy Dobeck – drums (1974-1987)
- Bob Pelander – keyboards (1976–87)
- Gary Markasky – lead guitar (1978–83)
- <u>Kevin Raleigh</u> – keyboards, vocals (1978–87)
- Michael Gismondi – bass (1979–87)
- Rick Bell – saxophone (1982–84)
- Danny Powers – lead guitar (1983–87)

The Michael Stanley Band released 11 albums from 1975-1986, nine of them being on (back then,) major record labels. They worked with some very well-known producers, engineers and audio mixers. They recorded in major recording studios. Thanks to Wikipedia for the statistics.

So why is it most of America at the time was finding the "heartland, working class" sound of John Mellencamp, Bob Seger, Bruce Springsteen, etc., and the most popular rock band in Cleveland was not being noticed anywhere else? This was a band that set local attendance records that still stand today for some of the venues that they played, yet, drive 90 minutes in any direction and they are playing small clubs and touring nationally as the opening act of host of semi popular bands during the 70's and 80's.

This was a very different situation to be in. Most bands that "make it" on the national scene always start small from somewhere, become the local heroes and then move on to national touring and radio airplay. This was not the case with MSB. Huge local following for many years (even today, Mr. Stanley still plays about a dozen shows a year and they always have a nice crowd), but not able to "break out" of the bar band/opening act label. Why was John Cafferty a national act and not MSB? They had national exposure through MTV, had 2 songs on the Billboard Top 40, several in top 100 over the years, so why not MSB?

The rest of this "self-indulgent" tale basically tells my story of how I spent some of my youth trying to follow the elusive MSB from a home base in suburban NJ, and the incredible effort it took to become a follower of MSB, and how that carried into my adulthood, and basically shaped my interest in pop music.

Chapter Two
The Technology Dark Ages

The following, which most will find hard to believe, is 100% true. Anyone under 35 reading this, either as an E-BOOK, KINDLE, DOWNLOAD, or just plain old paper, will be stunned know that there weren't always 500 channels on the television, the internet and the world wide web, was just science fiction, and a phone was a large appliance that had cord attached to a wall, sometimes with a circular dialer that took forever to make a call with.

Most events and other daily occurrences appeared in what was then called a "newspaper" and evening news broadcast on one of the four channels our televisions had in the late 1970s.

So, how did this **"suburban boy who was suffering for art"**, find out about MSB and the great music they were putting out? Well, back in 1981 a new cable tv channel called MTV was launched and fortunately the local cable company (way before Comcast gobbled them up), carried this new channel in the summer of 1981.

I was a high school sophomore at the time and really had no interest in pop music at all. I actually preferred reading the encyclopedia, participating in sports and being a high school wallflower.

Fortunately, my high school alma mater, gave us a day off for some reason though I don't remember the exact day, maybe Columbus Day or something like that, all I do know that it was quite cool outside and I was inside the house.

I was in my parent's basement watching tv and I was punching the buttons on the cable tv box (didn't have a remote back then), the box had 64 channels 32 top/32 bottom, and I started watching MTV for some reason, Flock of Seagulls, Pat Benatar, etc., and then this catchy song came on.

I looked up and was amazed at the song and the visuals. This cool song and this group of guys working in a factory was the backdrop of the video. One scene of the factory crew, next scene of the same "crew" is performing as a rock band. 2 guitars, bass, 2 keyboards, drums, and sax. The front man with a cool leather jacket and beard, and the lead singer on this song had a perfect "mullet" (a look I could never achieve), and I thought to myself "how cool are these guys" they work in a factory and they play music on "the side". The song was truly "catchy", and really got my interest. There is also a "scene" in the video where the "factory crew" are now "working" in a hospital with the mullet guy as patient and the guy with the beard is a physician. I found it hysterical at the time. Then again, I was a teenager.

Little did I realize at the time they were a fulltime rock band and not factory/healthcare workers (lol). At the end of the video, I saw "**He Can't Love You" The Michael Stanley Band, Heartland, EMI America**. That's all I needed to know.

The rest of the day, I kept humming "**He Can't Love You, Like I Love You",** to myself. I was so motivated by the "working class" band that I went outside and starting chopping wood (no clue why, or what the song had to do with it). It was "motivating", the same way Rocky ran up the steps of the Art Museum. I thought this is what the other kids in school meant when they said "so and so is great" or "I can really relate to a certain song".

I was so not into "pop culture" I remember the year before, someone told me John Bohnam had died and I thought "who the hell is that"?

I went to school the next day and started asking anyone who would listen "Have you ever heard of the Michael Stanley Band". In Southern NJ, MSB was an unknown. Springsteen was still riding The River, Robert Hazzard was climbing the Escalator of Life, and Rick Springfield was dominating the local top 40. So, if I was going to seek out the Michael Stanley Band, I was going to do it alone.

After a couple more weeks MTV had stopped playing MSB in the rotation as more national and mainstream bands started to make videos and push the "original" MTV playlist out. There were plenty of other bands and music that caught my eyes and ears (more on that later), but MSB was "the one" that really got my attention.

"HE CAN'T LOVE YOU" VIDEO

"HE CAN'T LOVE YOU" VIDEO"

Chapter Three
The Mall, Sam Goody, And Where Is Heartland???

So, with MTV, and local radio out of the picture to track down MSB, what was I to do? Back in 1981 where did one go to find music? No downloads, no file sharing, so you head to the Deptford Mall and go to Sam Goody (which at one time was a large record store chain).

Not 100% sure, but I am pretty sure this was the first time I was in a record store. I do remember as a small child going to JM Fields (a department store back in the day) and buying a Beatles cover band album, which I thought was the real Beatles and it cost .99 cents. What a bargain shopper I was.

Once inside Sam Goody, I was quite confused where I would find "Heartland" the Michael Stanley Band album I was seeking. Would it be listed under "M" or "S"? I would be depending on my keen sense of knowledge to figure this one out.

Now I knew my father's high-end audio system did not have an 8-track tape player, so I knew that medium was out. As I scanned the walls of cassette tapes, I did not see the Michael Stanley Band anywhere. So, headed over to the shelfs of vinyl. First looking under "M", and being the quality speller, I was, I could not find it. So, sauntered over to "S" section and I found an album called "North Coast" by the Michael Stanley Band.

Whoa, I thought to myself the name fits, but who are the guys on the cover? Where is the guy with the beard? Where is the song "He Can't Love You"? Why is the album not called "Heartland"? Man was I confused.

I was unaware at the time that North Coast was actually the follow up to Heartland which came out in 1980, not 1981. Why MTV was playing a video from an album that was no longer current is beyond me. I often wondered as I got older why did the North Coast album not have a video? It had a couple singles released. So not being sure of what I was seeking, I decided against picking up "North Coast", since I did not want to be disappointed if it was not what I had envisioned.

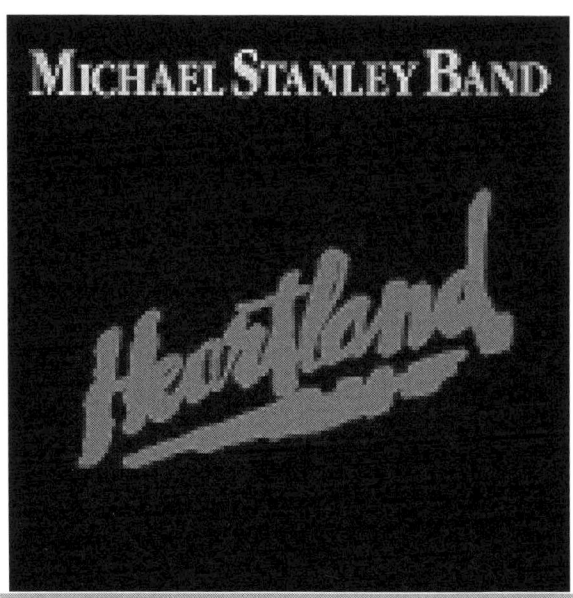

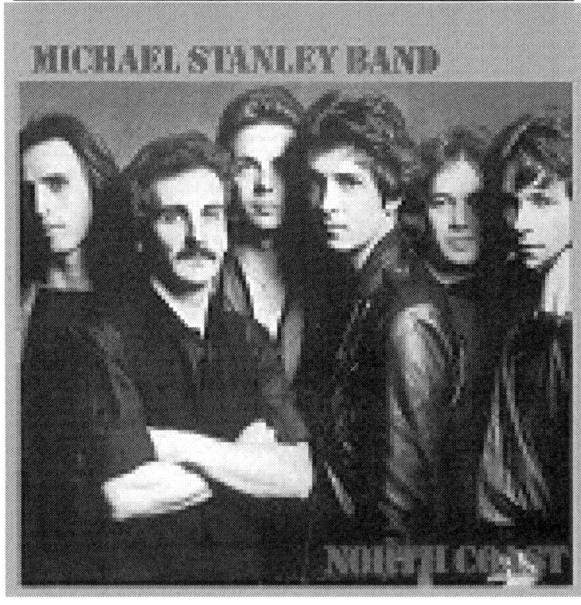

So, I left Sam Goody without "Heartland" and wondered if I would be able to find this album. So, I moved on and started discovering more MTV staples and listened to the radio more often to find that "sound" I was looking for. That would be the start of the "working class sound" that I would go on to appreciate for the rest of my life.

Chapter Four
High School Heroes No One Ever Heard Of

I spent the rest of my high school days being addicted to MTV. Mostly heavy metal pop type stuff Priest, Scorpions, Def Leppard etc. and of course working class sounds of Springsteen, Seger, Mellencamp. But I still sought out MSB.

School started in Sept 1982 and again I would quiz my classmates in regard to MSB. Still no one was aware of them. Fortunately, my good friend MTV once again provided me a connection to MSB.

I was really not a social person in high school, I knew everyone and everyone knew me, but the guys I hung out with were really more sports oriented than music related. So, after school and on weekends we would play basketball, tennis, or go to the movies while other kids had beer parties and girlfriends. Didn't hang with jocks or the brainiacs. Just those "in the middle" types. I was a guy who played football but was also an honor student. Not many of them when I was in high school.

The big positive that came out of that was I got to see MSB video for the song "Take the Time" one night on MTV. It was a country influenced song that talked about the blight of Americans in the early days of Reagan. The video was a western theme this time, the cool guy with the beard was wearing a cowboy hat and singing lead vocals. The guy will the mullet was singing backup harmonies. A little "tongue-in-cheek" humor at the end with a Clint Eastwood look-a-like dressed in the "Fist for of Dollars" garb with an orangutan (Every Which Way But Loose).

Wow... MSB was back. That of course meant another trip to Sam Goody, though "Take the Time" was not as catchy as Heartland's "He Can't Love You", I still found the song very listenable, so I had to get the album "MSB". This time finding the album was a lot easier than finding "Heartland". MSB was in big red letters on a black background, with the band's individual photos on the back cover. I also finally found the "Heartland" album at the time. So, I walked out of Sam Goody with "Heartland", North Coast, and "MSB". I had what I thought at the time the entire MSB catalog. Little did I know they had a greater history than MTV had provided.

I played the MSB album more times than I can remember. In addition to the Michael Stanley written/vocal tracks, Kevin Raleigh's "pop" oriented songs were really strong also.

I am sure my dad really hated the fact I used his high-end stereo/turntable, but that album became the "soundtrack" for my senior year in high school. Obviously, there were other influences (Survivor, Rick Springfield, J Geils, etc.). Unfortunately, the "Take the Time" video did not stay on MTV very long, the song and the rest of the MSB album continues to be my favorite work from the band.

As I got to listen to "Heartland" and "North Coast", I was coming to the realization, this band was quite talented, had a strong "working class" sound on all three albums. You can tell they were acknowledging their Cleveland roots, with songs like "In the Heartland", "Working Again", "Let's Hear It", etc.

So, the rest of the DTHS class of 1983 was rocking out to Journey, The Police, Def Leppard, etc. I was riding the MSB train by myself. I still had never heard the band on the radio, but I was sure that somewhere they had a following.

Chapter Five
Slippery Rock University And Pittsburgh

I graduated high school and went to college in Western Pennsylvania, at Slippery Rock University, and though my obsession with MSB was not a factor, I had hoped that being within 50 miles of Youngstown Ohio (a town that MSB often played and had a drinking age of 19), that perhaps I would be able to see the band or at least meet up with someone else who followed the band.

I moved into the dorm in late August 1983 and became a college student. First week I was there felt like a fish out of water, I was not prepared for the rural western PA "vibe" and struggled my first week.

Fortunately, I liked to work out and lift weights, while everyone else was out partying the first Friday of the new semester, I was in the basement of the dorm pumping iron (ok it was a Universal Gym), and a guy with a radio walked in and started working out also. The radio station was WDVE out of Pittsburgh, and then it happened. At first, I was stunned, then I was unsure of what I was hearing.

Oh, and this town

- is my town—PITTSBURGH!! alright?
- Love her, hate her--it don't matter
- 'cause I'm gonna stand and fight
- This town--is my town
- She's got her ups and downs
- But I love her, hate her--it don't matter
- 'cause this is my town

There it was, I had heard the Michael Stanley Band on the radio for the first time. The song was "My Town" and it was brand new to me (and later I would find out it was just released as the single to the album "You

Can't Fight Fashion"). It was a "rocking anthem", big drums and big guitars.

After all those years of never hearing an MSB song on the radio, I heard it and it was "customized", it was using the name Pittsburgh. I would later find out that My Town was customized to over 100 specific cities, so every major radio market had their own version of My Town.

Of course, the Slippery Rock area did not have cable TV yet so there was no MTV so I never saw the video while My Town was a "hit" single. I would eventually see the video on MTV back in South Jersey, and I thought it was really well done. It "portrayed" the band as kids playing in the garage, and then developing into a full-time band, with Cleveland as the backdrop. Years later I actually "chatted" with Bob Pelander's son via AOL messenger and I asked him if he was "the baby" in the video when Bob Pelander was playing basketball in the driveway.

In October of 1983, I was reading the Cleveland Plain Dealer and there was an article on MSB headlining a club tour to support You Can't Fight Fashion, and I see that they played the home city of Philadelphia on Oct. 11. **WTF!!!!!!!!!!!!!!!!!!!!!!** MSB played the home town and I was just finding out about it **AFTER** the fact. This was not a good day. Print media back in the day was very local and there was no way you could ever find out was happening in an area where you were not.

Fortunately, I knew someone who was affiliated with a local Philadelphia radio station and on October 4th, MSB played a LIVE radio broadcast from The Ritz club in NYC that was broadcast on WNEW out of NYC and WMMR out of Philadelphia live, so most of the Mid-Atlantic region got to hear the band, while the rest of the country would have to wait for the syndicated broadcast later. I was able to obtain a copy of the broadcast, with the legendary Dave Hermann doing the concert intro and I had my very first LIVE experience of MSB. **MSB Live at the Ritz** was a popular "bootleg" for those people who did not live in NE Ohio. Till this day, it might be the best quality and band performance I have heard. The band was on all cylinders that morning. This cassette tape was constantly played over the next 10 years. A few years ago, MS released a shorted version of the original on cd. The "talking" parts were edited out, in addition to the last song "Just How Good" was not included.

MSB also appeared on the national syndicated shows Solid Gold and American Bandstand. It seemed that maybe the rest of the country would finally get on the MSB train. Ah no.

The Cleveland Plain Dealer kept me informed sporadically about MSB, but when I left the area for any vacations, etc. I was "out of the loop" for MSB. That was always an issue.

At the end of spring semester 1985, I was driving back from Slippery Rock University and it's about a 6-hour ride back to NJ. So, I arrive home late in the evening and I get a radio station signal and I hear "If you ever wanted to see the Michael Stanley Band", and I was stunned and amazed at the same time. And then the radio spot was gone. I did not get to hear where MSB was playing.

A couple days later I found out that MSB had played Great Adventure Amusement Park in Jackson NJ, roughly 90 minutes from my home. Again, lack of having access to local media had prevented me from seeing MSB live. BUMMER!!!!!!!!!!!!!!!!!!!!!!!!!

After getting over the disappointment of missing MSB in Jackson, NJ, I was listening to WYSP in Philadelphia and then lightning struck.

Oh, and this town

- is my town—PHILADELPHIA!! alright?
- Love her, hate her--it don't matter
- 'cause I'm gonna stand and fight
- This town--is my town
- She's got her ups and downs
- But I love her, hate her--it don't matter
- 'cause this is my town

BANG!!!! MSB was being played on Philadelphia radio. My Town and the You Can't Fight Fashion album had fallen off the charts since 1983, but it was being played. MSB was now legitimate as far as I was concerned. When the song faded the DJ came on after and said "Great song about a great city by the Michael Schenker Group".

What???

Are you kidding me? MSB was now MSG? Now Michael Schenker is a quality musician (in the band UFO and his own solo projects), but did the disc jockey really make that mistake? Oh boy.

Later that summer on 1985, I wrote to Belkin productions (yes young people it was a letter) and got a nice reply from Susan Haffey who informed me that MSB really did not have much going on the rest of the summer. So, it would be another year of never seeing MSB live.

MSB will headline Spring Weekend

By KATHY ROTZ
Rocket Staff Writer

The Michael Stanley Band will be the feature band of this year's Spring Weekend, performing April 26 at 6:30 on the Union patio.

Marty Hahn, Union Program Board's concert committee's chairman, said that a variety of music is on the weekend.

The Romantics had been booked, but because of a recording company dispute, they had to pull out. Michael Stanley band was booked following this, Hahn said.

When the main band was chosen and the "blocks" were booked, filler bands had to be chosen, Hahn said. Filler bands were basically chosen to get a variety and familiarity of the music, Hahn said.

Earthwood and Norm Nardini and the Tigers, from Pittsburgh, have been on campus and have evoked good responses from students, Hahn said.

An informal survey of students was taken by UPB at the Union concerning the types of music that are popular and the responses, with the budget, were the deciding factors for the booking of the bands, Hahn added.

Spring Weekend also offers amusements, carnival games, movies, and various other entertainments throughout the weekend.

McManus added that the movies and various games are geared toward children to get the community, faculty, and staff, and the students to come together and have a good time.

THE MICHAEL STANLEY BAND

Chapter Six
April 26, 1986, A New Date That Would Live In Infamy.

After an uneventful end to 1985 I returned to SRU for the winter/spring term, little did I know 1986 would be the "breakthrough" year for myself and MSB.

I was walking through the student union and there it was. A poster on the wall advertising the Spring Weekend concert. April 26, 1986. The Michael Stanley Band was going to headline the concert. I was stunned and excited at the same time. Wow, I thought, after 5 years of the search, MSB was literally going to be playing "for me".

As the show approached, I often asked my fellow Slippery Rockers what they thought about the upcoming concert. SRU was primary a Pittsburgh town, so the enthusiasm was actually quite low. Donnie Iris was a Pittsburgh legend and even though he had played The Rock just a few years earlier, he was the preferred choice.

In addition to MSB, local Philly musician Tommy Conwell was also on the bill. Tommy had released "Walking on the Water" and it was getting a lot of Philadelphia air play, so students from the eastern part of the state were sort of enthused by that. So, the Pittsburgh fans and Philadelphia fans were not onboard for MSB.

I wondered to myself, would anyone care? SRU was not a popular choice for people from Ohio, and in the past SRU had hosted national acts like Joan Jett, John Cafferty, Eddie Money, Donnie Iris, John Parr and Vixen during my time there.

Of course, the three guys I lived with at the time two from NJ and one from PA, really were not enthused either, so get them "pumped up", we had to have an MSB after party in our apartment. I knew that would get them excited. In September we had a Born in the USA party to celebrate Bruce's Three Rivers Stadium show (which we did not attend), but we played Bruce all night, drank, danced and even broke out the indoor swimming pool (blow up kid's pool).

After quite a bit of anxious nerves (of course based on my past luck, I thought for sure the show would be cancelled), the day finally arrived. It planned to be a late afternoon early evening show, so the crowd would be lubricated enough after the earlier day's bands had already played.

The "stage" was actually the back patio of the student union. It was a medium sized brick outdoor pavilion type area that looked over a grassy field. Of course, I had already plotted my spot on the grass, and I also brought my boom box with me to record the show on cassette.

As it got closer to the start of the show, I thought to myself, you have to get "backstage" and meet the band. I didn't know how to go about it, but I decided to give it a shot.

I wondered around the student union looking to see where the band would be hanging out before the show. There were no dressing rooms, so they had to be in a classroom or conference room. I circled the first floor and ran into Tommy Conwell who was watching tv. I said hello and mentioned my excitement to see MSB and then maybe catch a bit of his show. Conwell chuckled and called Michael Stanley an "old fart". I immediately wrote off checking out Tommy Conwell's show. I had to find MSB.

I went past a conference room that had paper on the glass part of the door. This had to be the spot. I grabbed a pen off a table and ripped a piece of paper off the bulletin board. I thought for sure that burly security guards would be behind the door and prevent me from meeting the band.

I was really nervous for some reason; the five-year quest was coming to a potential end. I took a deep breath and opened the door and said "Hey guys, Tribe won today". I knew Michael Stanley was a big Indians fan and that would be my "in". Of course, it was still April and Cleveland were already playing terrible.

No security prevented me entering the room, I saw a huge tray of cold cuts and table full of coke a cola. That's it. No hot chicks, no crazy pre-show antics, etc. Very basic.

I went over to Michael, and said hello. He was very courteous. I asked for an autograph and he immediately signed. I said thanks, and stated I was from NJ and followed the band. He said thanks a lot. I circled the room and said hello to everyone else in the band and got their autographs also. I was quite enthused and now even more psyched to watch the concert. I said thanks again to the band and hoped they had a good show. Michael said thanks and that was it.

It was less than I expected, but then again they were just regular guys in their mid-30's, and probably made less money than my father did. Though like every band out there, they wanted the national attention and the financial rewards of that, but they were now just a "bar band" who were local heroes and trying to grind out a living. They were definitely the "working class, blue collar" band that performed music that I liked. In the 1980's music had become very flashy thanks to MTV, and these guys were no different than people I worked with over the summer at the supermarket, liquor store, etc. just better hair.

I went out back to where the patio was and I grabbed my spot. I was about 10 feet from the barrier wall. I set down the boom box, full of fresh batteries and a brand new 90-minute cassette ready to go.

The "upfront" crowd was definitely full of people from Ohio. It was a small crowd at first, and it started to grow as the countdown to start drew closer. The larger part of the crowd was in the back, where the "lubrication of the crowd" was heating up. Though SRU was an alcohol-free campus and the town of Slippery Rock was "dry", that never stopped The Rock crowd from having a good time.

The buzz of the crowd was building when the members of the crew finished the sound check, and then the members of the band filtered out onto the stage. The anticipation of the last five years was coming to an end.

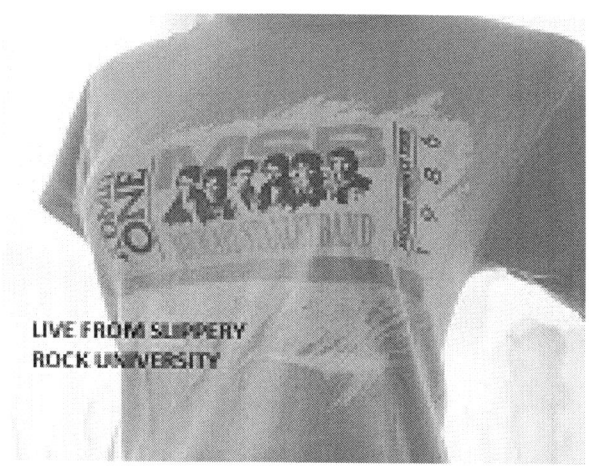

MSB PRE-SHOW?? WHO KNOWS????

Michael Stanley, Danny Powers, Michael Gismondi SRU 4/26/1986

MSB AT SRU
4/26/86

Dr. F. K. Szucs
Professor of Geology
Slippery Rock University
Slippery Rock, PA 16057

Chapter Seven
Let's Get The Show On The Road

"Its 10:35 in the heartland, make your move or you never will".

There it was, the first line from the song "In the Heartland" and MSB was playing live, and I was seeing them for the first time. The power of the opening chords, and the anticipation I was feeling was exactly as I thought it would be. Strong, powerful, the bass line thumping, and drums pounding.

"In the Heartland", was followed by "All I Ever Wanted" and then "Baby if You want to Dance", (which was a song I had not heard before, since it was on the Cabin Fever album).

Three songs in and MSB already had the crowd behind them. The band seemed to be in pretty good spirits (probably from the cold cuts tray).

Kevin Raleigh had the next song in the set with "Heart Says its Right", followed by another Stanley tune, "I'll Never Need Anyone More". Then there was an equipment malfunction and I thought, oh no, the MSB curse was going to continue. A brief break in the action, and the band was back to work.

The set list continued with "Midwest Midnight", "In Between the Lines", "When I'm Holding You Tight", "Spanish Nights," "Someone Like You", "Falling in Love Again" and a new song "Shut Up and Leave Me Alone" (which I would later find out was released on the 1984 album, 4th and Ten Live from Blossom).

The band was really rocking and the crowd, which had now grown quite large was really enjoying the music and atmosphere, since the weather was great (rare for Slippery Rock).

The awesome set continued with "Let's Get the Show on the Road", "Fire in the Hole" "Lover" "Somewhere in the Night", "He Can't Love You"," My Town" and finished off the concert with "Strike it Up" with Bob Pelander on the vocals.

It was GREAT. I had fulfilled a musical "bucket list" even before the term was invented. I had met, and seen MSB live. I had a quality live recording on cassette. Though 4/26 is my brother's birthday, but as far as I was concerned, it was MSB day.

After living the dream, we had the MSB after party and it was rocking also. I replayed the cassette that was recorded and the show was re-lived with a rowdy crowd of partiers and those who did not attend the show. At the end of the show Michael Stanley gave a shout out for his cousin Troy and praised the SRU crowd, which as documented by the cassette which I cherished for years.

MSB POST PARTY?? Who Remembers details!!!

After a non MSB summer, I returned to SRU in September and had a new group of guys to live with. Nicer apartment and no drama my previous roommates had created.

The Fall 1986 SRU crew

Again, living with non MSB fans, the last year of my college days again would be riding the MSB train all alone.

Since the town of Slippery Rock was pretty small, I had to go to a nearby small town of Grove City to check out any new vinyl. I had joined the college radio station the year before (WRCK), and I was fortunate enough to come across the 1985 charity record called "Eyes of the Children from C.A.R.E(Cleveland Artist Recording for Ethiopia). It was Cleveland's version of "We are the World". It was written by MSB and it was nice little ballad, that each member of the band had a few strong lines **("Before the grace of God go you and I")**. It also included other Cleveland musicians. This was another record/song I would have never have come across if not for just dumb luck.

Anyway, back in Grove City, I was looking through the local record store, and there it was. The latest album from The Michael Stanley Band. The album was "Inside Moves". Man was I excited. I snatched it right up and took right back to the SRU radio station to make a copy. I listened to it several times that day. It was a rocker. I was pretty pleased. "Show Me Something" and "Inside Moves" really stand out. The track "All is Said and Done" is also excellent. It was the first MSB record that did not have any Kevin Raleigh written songs since he joined the band. I could tell the album was sort of a "hodgepodge" of recordings from different time periods and not the usual go into the studio and crank it out. The cover of "Poor Side of Town" with Clarence Clemmons on sax was definitely a Heartland leftover. It was only released locally on the MSB label, and I thought at the time, that's not a good sign.

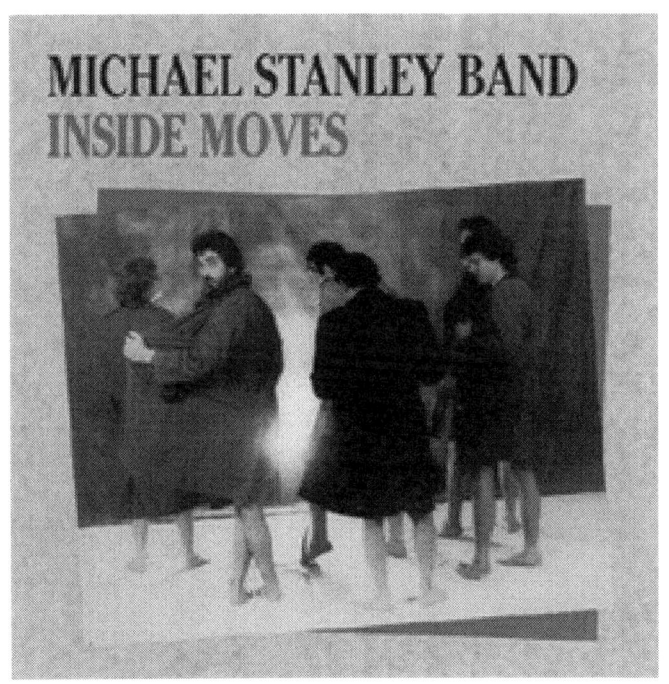

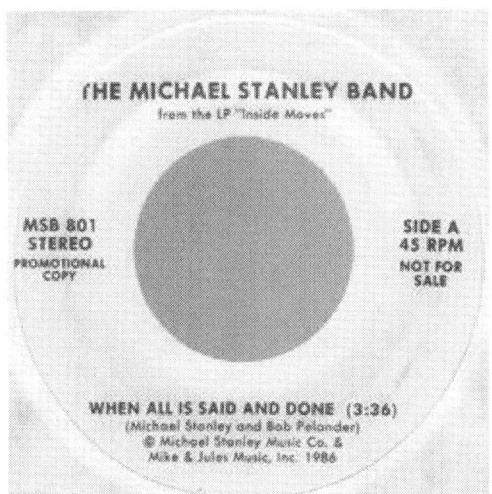

I was fortunate that I lived with a guy who had a girlfriend who went to Edinboro University which was up by Erie, PA. Their homecoming was in October and MSB was the headliner with Donnie Iris as the opener. Now I had often read about the MSB vs. Donnie battle, sort of like the

Browns vs Steelers. My roommate really liked seeing his girl so going up there was a no brainer, and she could get us discounted tickets.

So, after class on Friday October 17, we hit the road for Edinboro. Got there in the evening, and went to the local mall to kill sometime before we hit the Edinboro parties. Inside a record store at the mall, I was checking out the vinyl section, and I discovered the MSB album 4th and Ten. I had never heard of it before, let alone seen it. It was an odd-looking cover, but I had to snag it while I was there. I was not sure I would ever see it again. It was an album that was recorded during the 1984 Blossom Concerts. I would later find out it was self-financed as the band was trying to secure a new record deal. Not the best quality live album I have ever heard, but it was recorded in front of the hometown crowd.

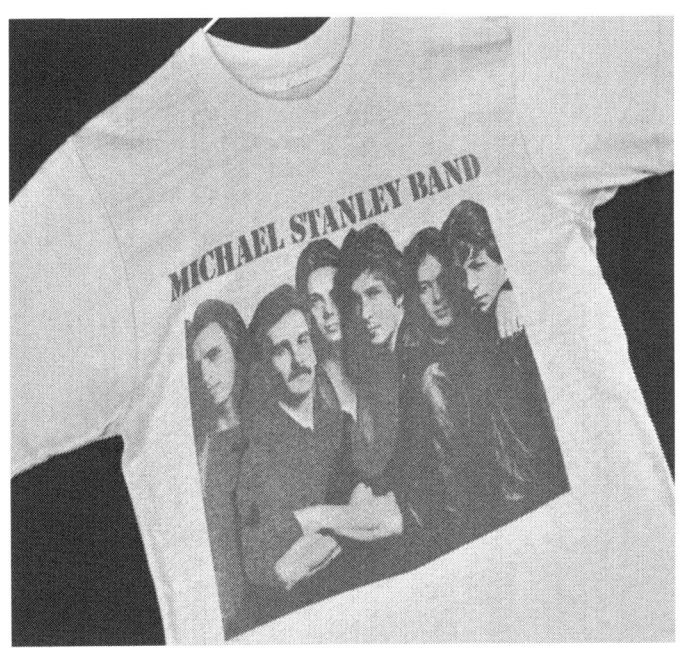

The next night we hit the Donnie Iris/MSB concert at Edinboro. I grabbed a discounted North Coast tour shirt from the vendor booth and went right up to the front of the stage. My roommate's girlfriend had invited a couple of her friends along also, so they went up front with me and those two sat in the back. I don't think they were really interested.

As usual Donnie Iris ripped it up, it was the third time I had seen him live and he always gives a good show. Then the strangest thing happened. The crowd started to leave. Not just the front stage area, but the entire auditorium.

WHAT??

I was stunned. I had been to several concerts over the years, but the opening act never over shadowed the headliner. Even when MSB came out they mentioned the Cleveland vs. Pittsburgh rivalry.

For the second time I was seeing MSB live, it was great show. We were right up front, one of the girls I was hanging with was really getting the band's attention. They played a few tunes off the new Inside Moves album, which was cool since those songs were not played at the SRU show in April, and they also added a sax player which also was not being used in the SRU show. Then I watched the most uncomfortable duet between two men I had even seen when Michael Stanley and Kevin Raleigh did a version of the song "Inside Moves". Both men dancing upfront and it was unflattering. By the end of the show the floor area was pretty empty and basically the "crowd" was upfront near the stage. It basically turned into a concert for the faithful. The band really tried to turn the crowd in their favor, playing all their well-known stuff, the Burgh fans were not buying.

Over all it was great show, though the crowd never really "got it to it", I would presume the homecoming parties were a bigger factor. Since I had already met the band, I really didn't bother to do the whole back stage meet and greet this time. As MS wrote in "Somewhere in the Night", "All you get is to keep are the memories, you got to make the good ones last". That was my mantra.

After the concert I went to an all-night outside rave, which was the first time I had ever been to one. It was great. It was kind of chilly out and good time had by all. After a quick early morning escape, we headed back to the Rock.

A few weeks later I was in the SRU library reading the Plain Dealer, and I saw an ad that stated **THE END OF AN ERA, THE FINAL BOW. WHAT!!!**

MSB was calling it quits and these were the final shows for the band. It was December 10 and the ad stated that there were 12 concerts scheduled and December 15 was the first one. I hustled back to my apartment, grabbed the phone started calling Ticketmaster. **ALL SHOWS SOLD OUT!!!!!!** I was stunned, I was leaving the next day for winter break and I had to head back to NJ. I had no contacts in Cleveland and of course back then only Ticketmaster and scalper were the ways to get tickets to an event.

Sadly, I drove back to NJ and once I was there, I frantically tried calling everyday seeing if any tickets were made available. Of course, they had not. I even tried to get a hold of a girl I knew lived in Northeast Ohio, whom I spent a short night with, and never called again. I was that desperate.

Unfortunately, I could not score any tickets, and none of my western PA friends were all that interested in spending their Christmas holiday hooking me up (thanks a lot).

I actually watched the Browns defeat the Jets on January 3rd 1987 hoping they would mention MSB on the broadcast, since that would be the final concert of the 12 concerts stretch. Alas they did not. After the New Year I read a nice article by Jane Scott in regard to the band and MS future. And that was it.

Years later I was able to secure a few recordings from the final shows, including the last one on Jan 3rd, and it sounded great. It was a real shame since the band sounded so good.

Even though I did not get to see the farewell shows, 1986 was a pretty good year in the Seeking Stanley Era.

END OF AN ERA!

MICHAEL STANLEY BAND
FAREWELL CONCERTS

THE RESPONSE WAS OVERWHELMING
3 SHOWS ADDED!!
DECEMBER 16, 17 and 29 - 8 P.M.

TICKETS STILL AVAILABLE FOR
DECEMBER 19, 20, 22, 23, 26, 27 - 8 P.M. • NEW YEAR'S EVE. DEC. 31 - 9 P.M.
NEW YEAR'S DAY, JAN. 1 - 8 P.M. • THE FINAL BOW, JAN. 2 - 8 P.M.

Reserved Tickets: $15.75 Available at the Front Row Box Office and TICKETRON
CHARGE BY PHONE WITH MASTERCARD OR VISA • Cleveland 524-0000 - Elsewhere in Ohio 1-800-362-0400

AFTER 13 GREAT YEARS IT ALL COMES DOWN TO ... 12 MEMORABLE SHOWS

Chapter Eight
What's Next For Me And MSB???

I graduated from Slippery Rock and pursued my career into adulthood and wondered what I would do without MSB? I read that Michael Stanley had become a local tv personality, hosting an evening magazine type show. He also starting working as afternoon drive DJ for a Cleveland radio station.

I went back to my music roots of Springsteen, Seger and Mellencamp. John Cafferty, The Hooters, Southside Johnny, Little Steven etc.

In 1987 I came across two cassettes that were compilations of MSB from the CBS/EPIC years (Band of Gold) and from the EMI America years (The Best of The Michael Stanley Band). I was hoping that was a sign of maybe something was coming down the pike. Alas, I was incorrect.

In another stroke of dumb luck, I was dating a girl who lived near Pittsburgh and we were at an area mall, and as always, I was perusing the stacks, and I came across a VHS called SONY VIDEO LP MICHAEL STANLEY BAND. Whoaaaaaaaaaaaaaaaaaaaaaaaaaaaaaaaaaa.

Who knew this even existed? I had scoured the record stores for years and never ever even got a whiff of this rare find.

Again, I snatched it up without any hesitation. The VHS contained the three MTV videos in addition to a live concert from Blossom that was obviously was promoting the North Coast material. The editing was not very good, but then again it was recorded in 1981. It was a pretty good find. The girl I was with tried to sway me into not buying it, but that was not happening, only to find out later she had it custom ordered and gave it me later as Christmas gift. (Till this day, I still have a sealed copy of the VHS) We of course broke up a short time later. LOL.

SONY

Video LP

MICHAEL STANLEY BAND

VHS hi-fi
(Mono compatible)
72 MINUTES

MICHAEL STANLEY BAND

HE CAN'T LOVE YOU
Kevin Raleigh (Bema/Kejra Music Co.) 3:35
© 1980 EMI-America Records, a division of Capitol Records, Inc.

TAKE THE TIME
Michael Stanley (Bema/Michael Stanley Music) 5:34
© 1982 EMI-America Records, a division of Capitol Records, Inc.

MY TOWN
Michael Stanley (Bema/Michael Stanley Music) 3:56
© 1983 EMI-America Records, a division of Capitol Records, Inc.

IN THE HEARTLAND
Michael Stanley (Bema/Michael Stanley Music) 3:28

I'LL NEVER NEED ANYONE MORE THAN I NEED YOU TONIGHT
Michael Stanley (Bema/Michael Stanley Music) 2:59

WORKING AGAIN
Michael Stanley (Bema/Michael Stanley Music) 4:59

WE CAN MAKE IT
Kevin Raleigh (Bema/Kejra Music Co.) 3:13

WHEN YOU'RE HEART SAYS ITS RIGHT
Kevin Raleigh (Bema/Kejra Music Co.) 3:38

HEAVEN AND HELL
Michael Stanley (Bema/Michael Stanley Music) 3:38

DON'T YOU DO THAT TO ME
Kevin Raleigh (Bema/Kejra Music Co.) 3:31

LOVER
Michael Stanley (Bema/Michael Stanley Music) 5:11

SOMEWHERE IN THE NIGHT
Michael Stanley (Bema/Michael Stanley Music) 3:53

DON'T STOP THE MUSIC
Michael Stanley (Bema/Michael Stanley Music) 4:32

HE CAN'T LOVE YOU
Kevin Raleigh (Bema/Kejra Music Co.) 3:56

PLAY A LITTLE ROCK AND ROLL (CUT THE B.S.)
Michael Stanley (Bema/Michael Stanley Music) 3:54

Executive Producer—Mike Belkin
He Can't Love You—Directed by Chuck Statler
Take The Time—Directed by Mark Robinson
My Town—Directed by Michael Collins
Concert Director—Chuck Statler
© 1981 M&B Joint Ventures

The copyright proprietor has licensed the program contained in this videocassette for private home use only, and prohibits any other use, copying, reproduction, or performance in public in whole or in part.
Sony is a registered trademark of the Sony Corp.
Video LP is a trademark of the Sony Corporation of America.

A Video LP™ release of the
Sony Corporation of America

(Mono compatible)
72 MINUTES

In another trip out to Western, PA (I think it was for a friend's wedding), I was in a record store and came across an album called "Delusions of Grandeur", by Kevin Raleigh the vocalist/keyboard player for MSB. I turned the cover over and didn't really recognize any of the names. I was familiar with Neil Geraldo from Pat Benatar's band, but I expected to see more familiar names if it was the correct guy.

I bought the album and when I got it home and cracked it open and played it, I wasn't sure what I was hearing, it sounded nothing like Kevin Raleigh's "sound" from MSB. Even within the liner notes, if it wasn't for the name Danny Powers, guitar player for MSB, I would never have thought this was the same guy who wrote and sang some great pop songs with MSB. "If You Love Me" from the MSB album is such a great, catchy song, the songs from "Delusions of Grandeur" are nothing like that. Not catchy, not pop oriented. It kinds of reminds me of how I liked Rick Springfield's catchy pop songs and then when he decided to change "his sound".

So "Delusions" quickly fell off the turntable, and I reverted back.

Also, that year I came across a book by Stephen King called "IT". I was never a big reader of horror, but in the intro Mr. King quotes the MSB song "My Town". Though he got the quote wrong, I thought it was pretty cool that a very popular author was recognizing MSB.

"This old town been home long as I remember

This town gonna be here long after I'm gone.

East side west side take a close look 'round her

You been down but you're still in my bones."

—The Michael Stanley Band

Dave Marsh, a noted music writer and author in his 1989 book "The Heart of Rock and Soul, 1001 Greatest Singles Ever Made" included MSB song

"My Town" as the 266th greatest single ever recorded. Again, it was nice that a well-known national writer included MSB in his list.

266 MY TOWN, The Michael Stanley Band
Produced by the Michael Stanley Band and
Bob Clearmountain; written by Michael Stanley
EMI-America 8178   1983   *Billboard:* #39

267 SMALL TOWN, John Cougar Mellencamp
Produced by John Mellencamp and Don Gehman; written
by John Mellencamp
Riva 884202   1985   *Billboard:* #6

I guess there are people who grew up in the despised places of America, small and large, who are immune to the pull of hometown patriotism, but it's unlikely that any of them have made rock and roll anthems. And for that matter, why restrict it to the States? Remember that guy who sang about how little a poor boy could do in "sleepy London town"? Or the ones who fashioned some of their best hits out of nostalgic remembrances of sights and sounds in Liverpool?

The kind of heartland rock and roll in which guys like Mellencamp and Stanley specialize has never been any more fashionable than the kind of places where those guys grew up. Coming of age in southern Indiana and northern Ohio, Mellencamp and Stanley were undoubtedly set upon with some frequency as disloyal long-haired louts, yet each of these rockers remained steeped in the sensibilities of his environment. John Mellencamp made it big; Michael Stanley barely made it at all. No matter where they went, their hearts never left.

Ties to home can be stultifying and dangerous. But understanding that the cosmopolitan values of media capitals like New York, Los Angeles, and London aren't the only way to look at things can also be liberating. And in the end, everyone knows this. Listen to a bunch of New Yorkers doo-wopping on the block or watch the eyes of a native Californian while some Beach Boys hit is spinning.

"My Town" and "Small Town" are rough and ready, defensive about their topic and yet dramatically assertive. Mellencamp's record perfects his latter-day folk-rock (C&W instruments played Rolling Stones-style); Stanley's is the one disc where Cleveland's favorite son got all the details of his Springsteen-meets-Cheap Trick synthesis just right.

"Small Town" taps into a lot of sentimental nonsense derived from America's myth of agrarian pastoralism. But play this record for an audience reared in Brooklyn and they'll tell you that growing up there felt the same way to them, because the way Mellencamp means it, a

A few years went by and I was phasing out my vinyl collection and trying to replace everything with compact disc. Most well-known bands stuff was available, Springsteen, Seger, Mellencamp, etc. Even John Cafferty was available. But not MSB.

In 1991 a very cool record label known as Razor and Tie re-issued Little Steven's classics. While I was pleased to see that, I was even more pleased to see R&T issued a "Best of" compilation of MSB on compact disc. It was called "Right Back at Ya". All the hits and almost hits on one cd. I snatched it up right away, and was thrilled to see liner notes written by Michael Stanley. Finally, I had some MSB on cd. Of course, even though I knew all the songs, no pops, scratches, or cassette hiss was a welcomed sound.

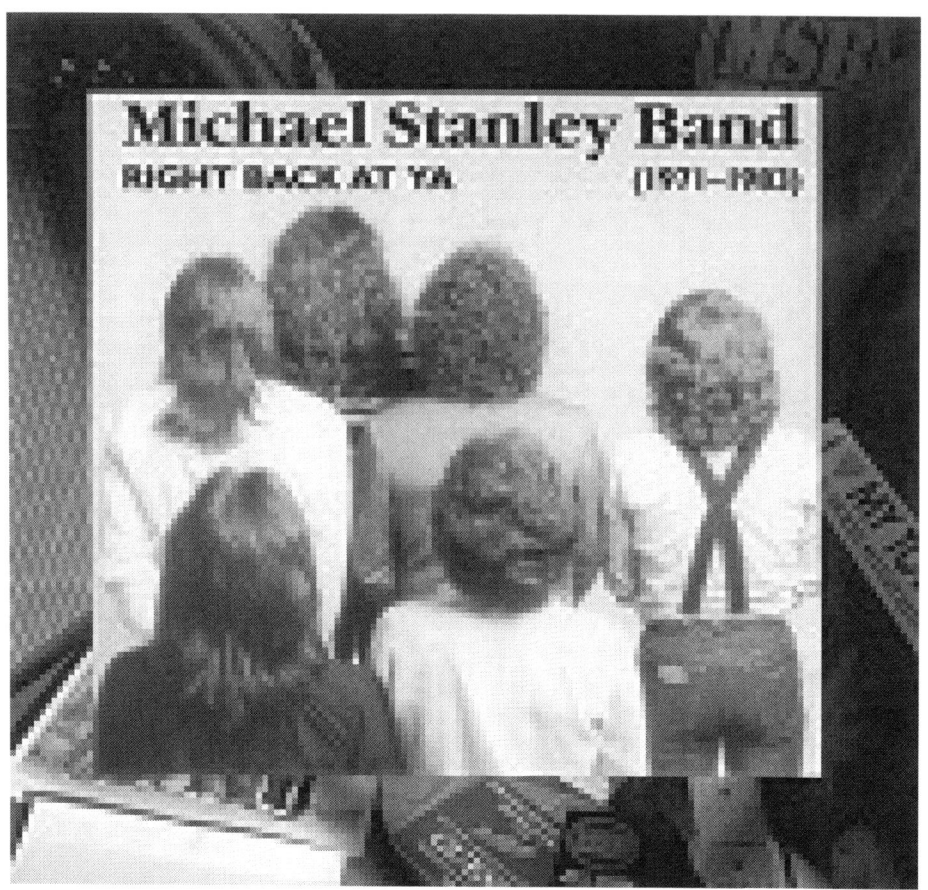

Shortly after the "Right Back at YA" cd came out, the fantastic folks at Razor and Tie re-issued the entire MSB back catalog. **WOW!!**

In addition to the re-issues, Heartland, North Coast, MSB, and You Can't Fight Fashion, all had bonus tracks that were culled from the Fourth and Ten Live album. **Excellent!!!!!!!!!!!!!!!!!!!!!**

Now I had the entire MSB collection, from the first Michael Stanley, Friends and Legends, You Break it You Bought It, Ladies Choice, Cabin Fever, and Greatest Hints. Though I really never cared for MSB of the 1970's, I chose to snag them all. Over time, Greatest Hints did grow on me, Last Night, and Beautiful Lies are great songs.

Though the EPIC years were not anywhere on my radar, the legendary live album called StagePass was issued on cd by Epic/CBS. I did get a copy because I am a completist, maybe played it a couple times, and then put it away. I know the Clevelanders consider it a great album, but not me.

Now in one form of another I had the entire Michael Stanley catalog on cd or vinyl. I had enough going on to be satisfied.

A year or so later, I was perusing a record store in the Deptford Mall, and as usual I check the "S" section looking for any Stanley offerings. Nothing listed, but I notice something out of place. A cd called THE GHOST POETS was in the section. Why I thought? Stock in the wrong spot I presumed. I took a closer look and the cover photo clearly has Michael Stanley and Bob Pelander on the cover.

The cd was not an MSB, since it included Jennifer Lee and original MSB member Jonah Koslen (who I never really cared for), but was a quality release with some MSB influence, but was not the flat-out rocker I would have preferred. Liars Moon, and Casanova are pretty good tracks.

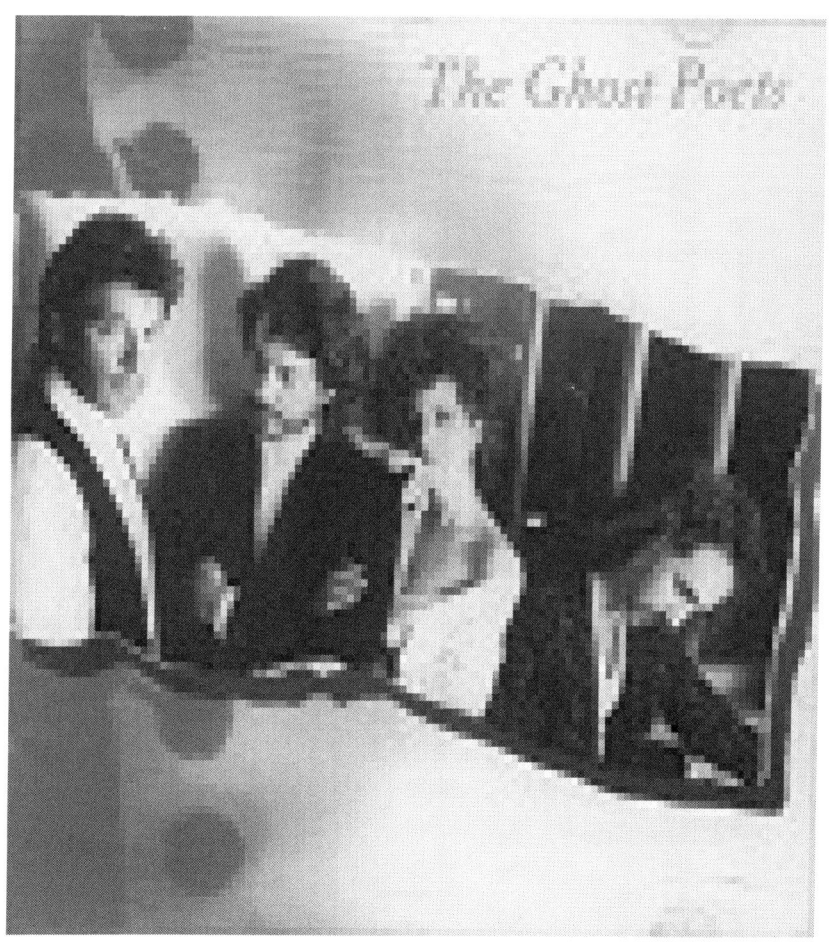

The Ghost Poets was a brief new addition to the Michael Stanley collection, it had a short life on the cd player. The back catalog was getting way more time especially the MSB album. This album/cd is far and away my favorite. I have often called the MSB album "true American music", its Americana before the term "Americana" was even coined. It rocks in the beginning with "In Between the Lines", slows down in the middle with "Spanish Nights, and One of the Dreams" and ends with a classic country flavored track called "Take the Time".

A lot of people will say "Heartland" is the best MSB album, and it's a great release, but as I stated MSB sealed the deal.

Chapter Nine

THE INTERNET BRINGS TOGETHER THE FAITHFUL

In 1993 I took a job with a company that was really quite cutting edge with technology. There was this low rumble in the business world of this thing called the internet. The company I worked for was really "into" the World Wide Web and it allowed its employees access to a T1 internet connection. Most home computer users if that had internet access were using a dial up service such as AOL or CompuServe, at if you were lucky at 56kps.

That T1 speed allowed me to access remedial html web sites, newsgroups and mailing lists. Sometime in the mid 1990's a person named Shea, from somewhere in the Midwest, started the very first MichaelStanley.com website.

The website was pretty basic just text and some graphics, but the big attraction was the forum piece of the site. Here was a "site" that anyone with MSB knowledge could post any and all information in regard to Michael Stanley. It was great. After 30 years on this planet, I finally was able to find like-minded peeps that could relate.

The best part about the forum was that Michael Stanley would actually partake in the discussions and answer your questions. It was a lot of fun trying stump him. He also posted his personal email address. That was the ticket. He would fill in the forum faithful with some band related history, inform us on some of the current progress going on, and even offered some "swag" out of his basement. A great highlight was that I asked MS a question via email in regard to re-issuing the "Inside Moves" album on cd, and he replied. It was kind of a thrill 20 plus years ago.

```
From: MSBB@AOL.COM at INTERNET   3/20/96  4:10 PM
Priority: Normal
Receipt Requested
TO: Timothy Giles at ISIEMAIL
Subject:
------------------------------ Message Contents ------------------------------

TIM...THANKS FOR THE KIND WORDS...DON'T WORRY, I'LL GET RAZOR & TIE TO GET IT
OUT (WHENEVER)...KEEP ROCKING...MICHAEL STANLEY
```

Another thing the forum allowed me access to was the "Cleveland connection" for MS info. I was not aware that MS had a heart attack in 1991. I knew John Mellencamp had one in 1994, but I guess Rolling Stone missed Mr. Stanley's. I also was not aware that Mr. Stanley had divorced his first wife and married Wayne Newton's wife's sister, who also worked with him on the PM magazine show. It also introduced me to Dave_From_Akron, who would later become a huge source of MSB related recordings and videos that no one other than someone "inside" would have access to. We were able to swap stuff I had acquired with his collection. It was pretty cool.

In 1996 the first Michael Stanley solo cd "Coming Up for Air" was released on Intersound records (RIP). In true Michael Stanley fashion, the cd was "interactive" (pretty high tech for the time) but was flawed. Most people that put it into their Win95 computers found that it did not work correctly. This was really designed for Macintosh, but since I worked in tech I was able to get it to work within Windows. It was pretty cool. The music was decent (After Hollywood and Coming Up For Air), but to me it was kind of a disappointment.

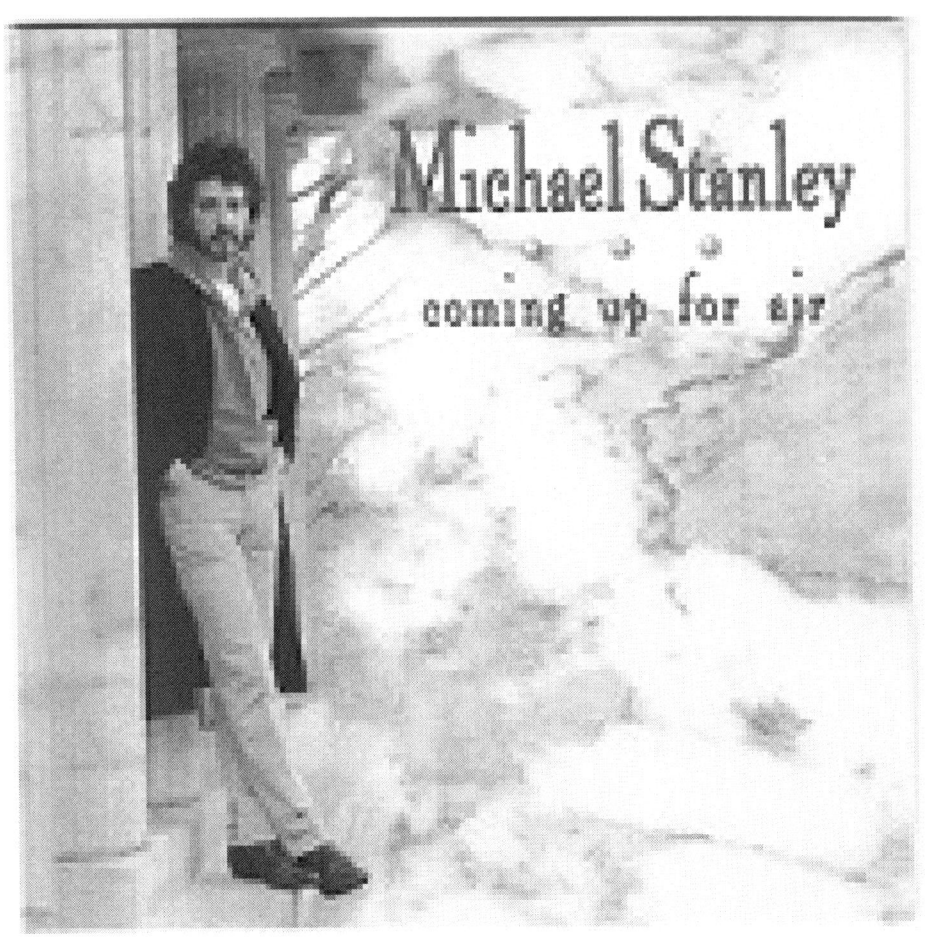

In 1997 that great peeps at Razor and Tie again came through with another MSB compilation "Misery Loves Company" which highlighted the songs that were not well known, but I really enjoyed the selections. This also included MS written liner notes, which is always a nice addition to a cd. I feel that some of MSB's best stuff was included on this cd.

A huge factor in addition to the MS website was EBAY. I was constantly purchasing rare items that I was not aware of existed. Most of it was memorabilia such as posters, clothing or rare audio/video recordings.

One of the most awesome items I was able to grab on EBAY was a t-shirt from the Final Bow Last shows from 1986. Though I knew I would never wear a man's small, I knew one day I would pass it on to my future son, where he could say "Who the hell is Michael Stanley"?

Another rare item at the time was a video done by the Cleveland Browns and United Way doing a sort of fantasy story (think Lord of The Rings with no budget), with MSB doing the soundtrack with a great song called "Hard Die the Heroes". Cheesy story, great song.

In my opinion the greatest EBAY find was the "first official" MSB offering on cd. The album "Inside Moves" on cd was issued for one the early reunion shows that was sold at the concert. It was pressed on the MSB label. To me this was the holy grail of MSB stuff.

I even picked up a cd from a company called Little Fish that included a track from an MSB cover band called Stage Pass, the song was called "On the Radio". Reminds me of Cabin Fever version of MSB.

In 1998 those great peeps at R&T released Michael Stanley's acoustic CD "Live in Tangiers", which was basically MS on acoustic guitar recorded at a club in Akron, OH. named Tangiers. It was a nice little cd with some of the MSB staples done acoustically.

Through the website I found out that MS would be playing the Nautica Stage in the Flats area of Cleveland in June 1998. I had now been married for a few years and my wife Donna had accepted the MS obsession, (maybe tolerated is a better word). My wife was also interested in the Amish lifestyle, so what better way to scratch off another bucket list would be to go the Cleveland and see MS in front of the hometown crowd and cruise through Holmes County Ohio and check out the large Amish population there.

We made the drive out there, PA turnpike, to the Ohio Turnpike, beautiful scenery, nice weather, etc. Spent one day in Holmes County, dropped a fortune in Lehman's, and did the whole tourist thing.

The next day we hung around Cleveland, checked out "The Jake", The Rock Hall, Sea World, etc. We went down to the Flats area, and hit Nautica. We had a pretty good spot to watch the show, and waited with anticipation for the show and more importantly the crowd.

The show was billed Michael Stanley and Friends. A local band was the opening act, and then MS came out and basically did an acoustic show with not a lot of electric. It also rained off and on during the show. Though it was a "nice" set, I found it a little disappointing that it was not a full-fledged rock and roll show. I was surprised that the crowd also was not really "into it". The vibe in the beginning of the evening really didn't live up to the "hype" that I guess I presumed would have happened. I guess reading and hearing Blossom shows from the past may have clouded my expectations.

MS and the band **"played all the hits you want to hear"**, but in an acoustic format. Of course, it was the 1990's where it seemed all the 1980's rockers were trying to re-invent themselves, or put a new spin on the old stuff. My wife enjoyed the fact they played "Take the Time" so she was content with the show and all the Amish crap she got to take back to NJ.

The 1990's continued when MS wrote a song for the Cleveland Browns who were returning to NFL after the "original" Browns moved to Baltimore and became the Ravens. It was sort of a "who's who" in Cleveland music participating in the song with many former Browns players and Clevelanders participating in the video. It was by far the best thing MS had written since "Inside Moves". It was flat out anthem type rocker. I thought for sure it would go national or get some love from ESPN. In true MS fashion, it did not (grrrrrrrrrrrrrrrrrrrrrrrrrrrrrrr).

Fortunately, the decade ended with MS doing his annual New Year's Eve Cleveland show. MS then offered a cd of the show to those who were in attendance, and a few copies available to those not in the 216-area code. That would be me. MSLIVE2K was recorded live with basically the same band whom I saw in 1998, but it was not an acoustic show. Over all not a bad live cd recorded in a bar.

Michael Stanley & Friends
Recorded Live At The Odeon
Cleveland, Ohio
12•31•99 / 1•1•00

Michael Stanley • *Lead Vocals / Guitar*
Bob Pelander • *Keyboards / Vocals*
Tommy Dobeck • *Drums*
Jennifer Lee • *Vocals / Percussion*
Marc Lee Shannon • *Lead Guitar*
Rodney Payka • *Percussion / Vocals*
Eroc Sosinski • *Bass / Vocals*
Cy Sulak • *Lead Guitar*
Paul Christensen • *Sax*

RAIN OR SHINE
BELKIN & BUD LIGHT
PRESENT
MICHAEL STANLEY
NAUTICA STAGE
SAT JUN 13 1998 8:00 PM

SEC 1 — N 25 A — 29.00
SEC 1 — N 26 A — 29.00

CHAPTER 10
WILL THE RIDE CONTINUE?

After surviving the Y2K scare, and managing to get through the depressing music of the nineties without committing suicide, I was coming to a cross roads myself. So far the Michael Stanley of the 1990's was not really what I needed. Though I continued to appreciate Michael's solo stuff, every new cd had a couple decent tracks, the whole band "sound" I felt was lost with the home recording, the self-producing and having his best friend Bill Szymcyk working as the second "set of ears".

Since I appreciated the "Heartland" sound, I gravitated to 1990's country. Garth Brooks, Toby Keith, Mary Chapin Carpenter, etc. became my "new music". I never cared for rap, and definitely hated grunge. You could hear 1990's country artists had grown up on 80's music.

In 2000 the cd 18 Down came out from those great peeps at Razor and Tie. Another decent release from MS, again a couple decent tracks, but overall it just didn't "grab me". The cover of "Downstream" and "Tremelo Parkway" are decent, but it seemed like MS was trying to do the "white boy suburban blues". Not really my thang.

In 2003 MS released the cd "The Ground" and this was a pretty quality release. The title track and "My Last Day on Earth" are truly great songs. I thought hey maybe this was the start of the "sound" I would hope return. In addition, MS got some national attention when he appeared on the ABC sitcom, The Drew Carey Show. MS unfortunately had a pretty lame line to say, as opposed to Joey Ramone or Joe Walsh. But it was still cool to watch.

The following year, with the help of the internet I obtained a copy of Michael Stanley and The Resonators (the name of his new "live band") "Instant Live" cd. Instant Live was this new concept that the live show the audience had just seen could obtain a cd version of the concert an hour or so after the concert. No more waiting for the bootleggers or home tapers to get it out. It was a brief concept that was a great idea, but didn't not last long.

The Instant Live cd was recorded in Cleveland and included a lot of classic MSB stuff, some new stuff, and even had Kevin Raleigh guest on some vocals. It was definitely a nice piece of music. It was the concert I had hoped they had played when I went out to Cleveland in 1998. Give MS credit, he has a really good live band that he has been playing with for most of the 2000's.

The rest of the first decade on the 2000's added five more cd's to the collection. Nice stuff, a couple good songs on each cd, one cd of just covers of rare songs I guess MS really enjoyed doing. I would say that "American Road" is probably the next best cd of the first decade, after "The Ground". I personally feel that MS is just releasing too much filler and not enough quality stuff. But he owns the record label so its his show.

His label called "Line Level" did put out a DVD of a local Cleveland produced tv show MSB Confidential which shined a light on some of the band members thoughts of their experience with MSB. Another example of how the internet has played a huge part in being able to keep up with MS and what the NE Ohio folks have gotten to view.

Line Level also re-issued the Sony VHS on DVD, which was a welcomed addition, since using my VHS player was really starting to stink. Anything on DVD was better than VHS.

In addition, Line Level also issued a DVD of MS playing the Rock and Roll Hall of Fame acoustically, apparently right before "Live in Tangiers" was issued. Another interesting chapter in my journey that again, not aware was even happening. I understand his late wife was instrumental in a lot of the Line Level material that was being issued. For her involvement I am truly grateful, since it seemed via the web forum MS really did not want to be involved in any new technology. LOL.

The second decade of the 2000's has so far released 6 new cd's. Again, some quality music, and some not. My personal favorites "The Hang" and "The Job".

Thanks to the internet, keeping track of MS the last few years has been much easier than in the early days. Facebook has a few user groups that keep track of MS. Google MS name and you get hundreds of responses. All of his work at one time or another has been available on Amazon, and now via the Line Level web site. Over the years a few people have assisted with putting out MS authorized live recordings, both audio and video.

Thanks to internet streaming, I will often listen to MS doing his radio broadcast on WNCX out of Cleveland. As of today, he still plays some concerts every year in the NE Ohio area, recently came through a quadruple bypass surgery. The Cleveland Plain Dealer also keeps me informed on any news involving MS, mostly reviews of his cd's or local concerts.

I personally have passed the half century mark in my time on earth, and spend most of my time these days with my wife and son. MS has taken a backseat in my life over the past 10 years or so. I often look back at my younger days and wondered why I spent so much effort tracking MSB. Its funny because I seemed to be drawn to musicians and bands that never really became popular. Southside Johnny, Little Steven, John Cafferty, etc. all had a national attention, but never became as popular as Springsteen, Seger, Mellencamp, etc. I must have had an affinity for bar bands.

Recently my brother sent me a text and stated "I have been listening to MSB lately on Amazon, and I can't believe they are not more popular, they have some good songs". And that my readers, pretty much sums everything up.

CHAPTER 11

We Sing With Our Heroes, Thirty Three Rounds Per Minute…….

Cleveland-based rocker, radio star, Michael Stanley dies at 72

ASSOCIATED PRESS

CLEVELAND — Michael Stanley, a Cleveland-based rocker who with his namesake band reached the Top 40 in the 1980s with the hits "He Can't Love You" and "My Town" before going on to a long career as a radio disc jockey, has died. He was 72.

Stanley died Thursday after a seven-month battle with lung cancer, his family said in a statement. The rock radio station WNCX in Cleveland, where he worked for 30 years, posted a message from Stanley himself, saying:

"Hey gang… Well, if you're reading this then I am off to catch up with that big club tour in the sky. But before the bus pulls out I wanted to thank all of you for being part of my musical journey, both on the stage, on record, and behind the microphone here at WNCX."

Accompanied by his signature, Stanley's send-off continued: "Somebody once said that if you love your job then it's not really work. And if that's true (and I definitely think it is) then I have been happily out of work for over fifty years!"

The Cleveland legend released his first album while still in college and formed the Michael Stanley Band in 1974. After a brief period of national popularity in the early '80s, sales fell off and the band broke up in 1987. Stanley, also a songwriter, continued to record and tour, and remained beloved in his hometown as a radio and television personality, performer and recording artist.

"He was so emblematic of that raging heart that doesn't care that it's gonna lose — it's still gonna leave everything on the field. And when he wrote those songs, those kids in a city where the river caught on fire and the lake died, they felt like their lives mattered," music critic and author Holly Gleason told Cleveland.com. "If you were a kid coming of age in Cleveland in the '70s or the '80s, he was our hand on the brass ring."

A private funeral for Stanley was planned.

CHUCK CROW, THE PLAIN DEALER VIA AP

Michael Stanley is shown in 2000 in Cleveland. The rock musician and radio disc jockey has died at age 72 after battling lung cancer.

Hey gang…

Well, if you're reading this then I am off to catch up with that big club tour in the sky. But before the bus pulls out I wanted to thank all of you for being a part of my musical journey, both on the stage, on record, and behind the microphone here at WNCX.

Somebody once said that if you love your job then it's not really work. And if that's true (and I definitely think it is) then I have been happily out of work for over fifty years!

Sure it would have been nice if this had all lasted a bit longer but my time on this mortal coil has been blessed with great family, friends, and co-workers and you can't ask for much more than that!

I would especially like to thank Bill Louis, Paula Balish and Tom Herschel for their friendship and support over these last months: they've gone out of their way to make this situation as workable as possible and I can only hope that you have friends like these surrounding you.

So thanks again, take care of yourself and each other and remember, now more than ever: it's your world…pay attention! Peace…

March 5, 2021, sadly has brought the ride to end. I have tears in my eyes as I type this, even though it has been more than six months since Mr. Stanley's passing. When I originally wrote this self-indulgent, let's have some fun and bring some laughs to the party novel about a high school kid's discovery about a semi-successful Midwest based rock and roll band, I really had no idea if anyone would really care to read about my little story.

As of November 2021, this story has sold quite a few copies and raised quite a bit of money for charity. When I told Mr. Stanley about the pay it forward portion of the program, he was greatly impressed. Amazon royalties have been donated to St. Christopher's Hospital for Children in Philadelphia, St. Jude's Hospital for Children in Memphis, The American Cancer Society, The Cleveland Food Bank, and even a GoFundMe for a fellow MS admirer. I am thankful to everyone who purchased an original edition of SEEKING STANLEY…

This epilogue is something I wanted to update and wrap a bow around this 40 year journey that Mr. Stanley and his music has taken me on. Yes he was Northeast Ohio's hometown hero, but he was also quite a co-pilot on long drives, late nights, and even a successful pick up line every now and then.

I have received quite a few emails over the last few years, as others have told me about their MSB/Michael Stanley tales as well. Some similar to mine, other just Cleveland folk who got on the band wagon early, and stayed for the entire ride.

So my friends, I leave you with a final question that has been eating at me for years…

IS ALL I EVER WANTED OR SPANISH NIGHTS THE BEST SONG EVER WRITTEN BY MICHAEL STANLEY GEE?

FROM MR. STANLEY HIMSELF 10/2/2018

Tim...

   Well, I can honestly say that I didn't see this one (your book) coming but it has brought a lot of laughs and smiles to the party: hats off to you! I appreciate you sending a copy my way but I have to admit that after someone in my band alerted me to it's existence I had already ordered a copy (and will now pass this one on to Pelander or Dobeck or some other appropriate dude from the cast of characters.)

   Your diligence and tenacity (where fandom is concerned) is greatly appreciated and I certainly hope you've enjoyed the ride. My favorite line in the whole thing is your description of "the most uncomfortable duet between two men that I had ever seen"...I nearly did an old fashioned spit take on that one! And to answer you question, I have no issues whatsoever with the project... but thanks for taking the time to make it happen and hopefully during your quest you weren't physically abused by the Bruce and Bon Jovi crowds.

   I hope all is well in your world and thank you again (from the leader of america's most successful unsuccessful band) for putting it all down on paper!

Peace...Michael Stanley

Thank you to Anna and Sarah and your families.

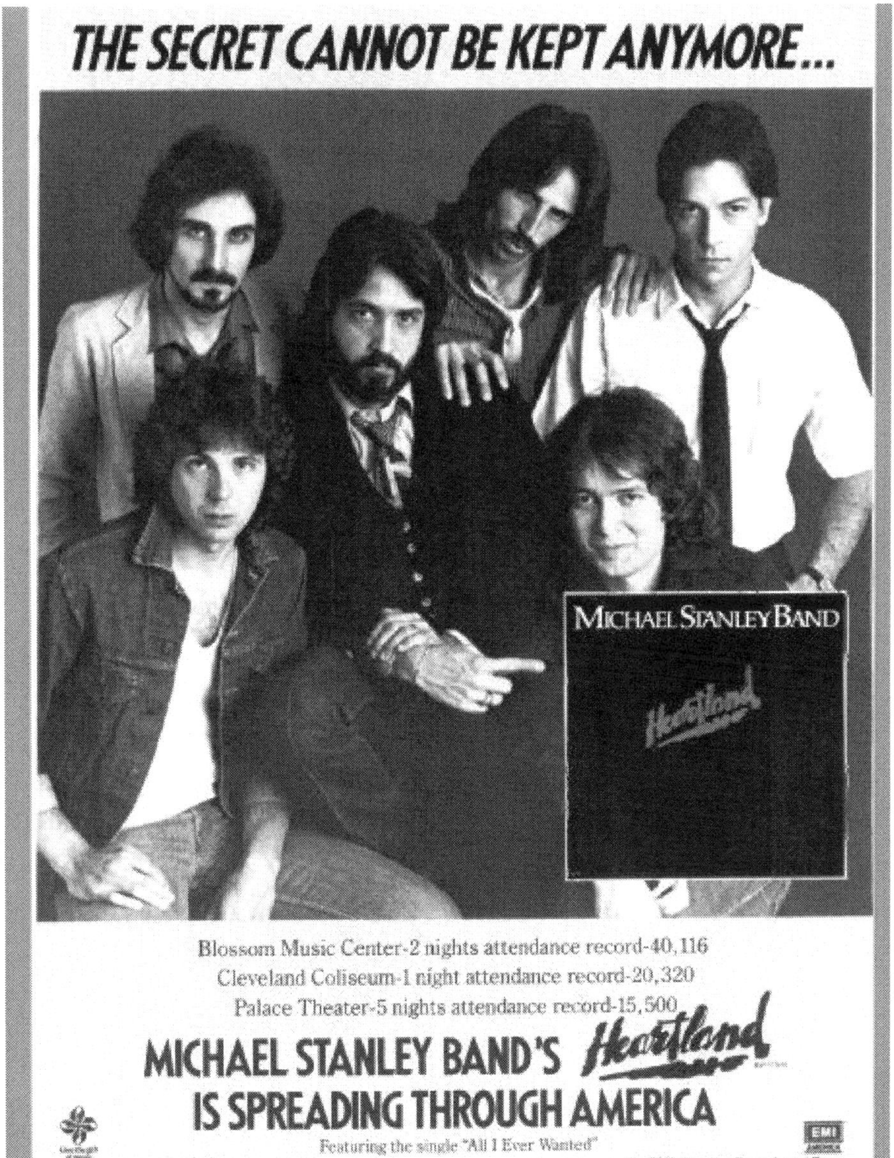
THE SECRET CANNOT BE KEPT ANYMORE...
MICHAEL STANLEY BAND
Heartland
Blossom Music Center-2 nights attendance record-40,116
Cleveland Coliseum-1 night attendance record-20,320
Palace Theater-5 nights attendance record-15,500
MICHAEL STANLEY BAND'S Heartland
IS SPREADING THROUGH AMERICA
Featuring the single "All I Ever Wanted"
Produced and arranged by The Michael Stanley Band
EMI AMERICA
On EMI-America Records and Tapes

Made in United States
Orlando, FL
14 March 2023